Survey Responses From Region 3:
Are We Achieving the Public's Objectives for Forests and Rangelands?

Michelle Haefele, Deborah J. Shields, and Donna L. Lybecker

I0410849

U.S. Department of Agriculture   Forest Service

Haefele, Michelle; Shields, Deborah J.; Lybecker, Donna L. 2005. **Survey responses from Region 3: Are we achieving the public's objectives for forests and rangelands?** Gen. Tech. Rep. RMRS-GTR-156. Fort Collins, CO: U.S. Department of Agriculture, Forest Service, Rocky Mountain Research Station. 27 p.

Abstract

The survey on values, objectives, beliefs, and attitudes, implemented as a module of the National Survey on Recreation and the Environment, asked over 7,000 respondents nationwide about their *values* with respect to public lands, *objectives* for the management of these lands, *beliefs* about the role the USDA Forest Service should play in fulfilling those objectives, and *attitudes* about the job the agency has been doing. This report—one of a series of similar regional reports—shows the attitude of respondents from the Southwest (USDA Forest Service Region 3: Arizona and New Mexico) is less favorable toward the Forest Service performance concerning the restricting of mineral development on forests and grasslands than respondents from the rest of the United States. Nationwide, as in the Southwest, the most important objective was conserving and protecting forests and grassland watersheds.

Other reports in the series *Are We Achieving the Public's Objectives for Forests and Rangelands?*

- *Survey Responses From Region 5* (California and Hawaii) RMRS-GTR-157

- *Survey Responses From Region 8* (Alabama, Arkansas, Florida, Georgia, Kentucky, Louisiana, Mississippi, North Carolina, Oklahoma, Puerto Rico, South Carolina, Tennessee, Texas, Virginia) RMRS-GTR-158

- *Survey Responses From Region 9* (Connecticut, Delaware, Illinois, Indiana, Iowa, Maine, Maryland, Massachusetts, Michigan, Minnesota, Missouri, New Hampshire, New Jersey, New York, Ohio, Pennsylvania, Rhode Island, Vermont, West Virginia, Wisconsin) RMRS-GTR-159

- *Survey Responses From the Intermountain West* (Arizona, Colorado, Idaho, Montana, Nevada, New Mexico, Utah, Wyoming) RMRS-GTR-160

- Comparison of 2000/2003 Data – Forthcoming

Survey Responses From Region 3: Are We Achieving the Public's Objectives for Forests and Rangelands?

Michelle Haefele, Deborah J. Shields, and Donna L. Lybecker

Contents

Introduction

The mission of the USDA Forest Service is twofold: caring for the land and serving people. Because satisfaction is an individual concept with multiple facets, providing high quality customer service and achieving high levels of customer satisfaction can be as complex and challenging tasks as is managing for healthy ecosystems.

A person's attitudes about the Forest Service are often influenced by the nature and outcomes of his or her interactions with Forest Service employees. Were they polite, knowledgeable, helpful, and professional? Was the process straightforward, efficient, prompt, and fair? Was the desired outcome achieved, such as acquiring a fuelwood permit or getting information on day hikes? Although traditional customer satisfaction surveys do a good job of collecting this type of information, they tend to focus on delivery of services to specific classes of "users" (permittees, applicants for timber sales or grazing allotments, etc.), and are not designed to capture the preferences and attitudes of the broader public.

In addition to personal interactions with the Forest Service, people's perceptions of the agency are also influenced by their attitudes about how and toward what end we manage the land. The agency and various segments of the public have both general, and in some cases quite detailed, objectives related to the health of forests and rangelands, how Forest Service lands should be managed, and the activities that should be allowed to take place on them. If stakeholders observe that an objective they deem important is not being fulfilled, their satisfaction with the Forest Service may be lower, regardless of the quality of their interactions with individual Forest Service employees or their experience with agency protocols. Gaining an understanding of the public's objectives and their consistency with agency objectives, or lack thereof, can provide useful input to the strategic planning process.

The agency's goals and objectives are embodied in the 2000 Strategic Plan. Information on the public's goals and objectives has been collected through an ongoing survey entitled "The American Public's Values, Objectives, Beliefs, and Attitudes Regarding Forests and Rangelands" (hereafter VOBA). The VOBA survey asked respondents about their environmental values as they relate to public lands, their objectives for the management of forests and rangelands in general, as well as those managed by the Forest Service, their beliefs about whether it is the role of the Forest Service to fulfill those objectives, and their attitudes about the performance of the agency in fulfilling their objectives.

Data and Methodology

Objectives Hierarchy

The VOBA survey's objectives, and related belief and attitude statements, do not ask respondents about their opinions of the goals in the Forest Service Strategic Plan. Nor do they ask for an individual's reaction to the Chief's Agenda or Leadership Team priorities. Rather, the VOBA survey's objectives statements were developed during a series of 80 focus group meetings conducted with members of various stakeholder groups as well as individuals throughout the country. As such, they represent the main objectives for land management as they were presented to us by the public.

An objectives hierarchy was constructed for each focus group. These hierarchies indicated goals each group or individual had for the management of forests and rangelands, and how they would like to see each goal or objective achieved. These objectives ranged from the abstract strategic level to the more focused or applied means level (see figure 1).

Within the objectives hierarchy, the strategic level is an abstract objective. Fundamental-level objectives represent a context-specific application of strategic objectives. End-state fundamental objectives represent the desired state of the world. Fundamental means

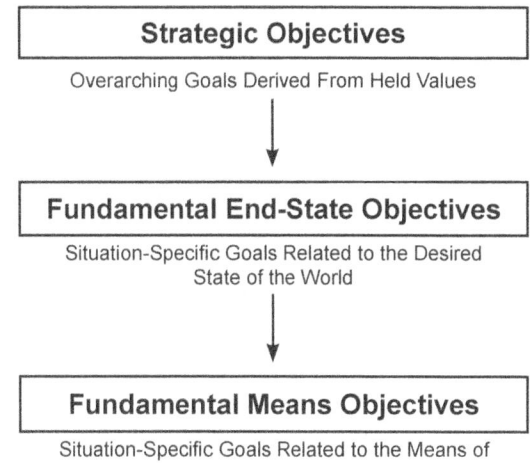

Figure 1—Objectives Hierarchy.

objectives capture the methods by which the desired end state should be achieved.

VOBA Statements

The objectives elicited from all the focus groups were pooled, duplications eliminated, and overlaps reorganized. The 30 remaining items formed the fundamental objectives that indicate both end-state preferences and the means by which they should be achieved. Each correlates to one of the strategic objectives. Five strategic-level objectives were consistently revealed by the focus group participants: Access, Preservation/Conservation, Economic Development, Education, and Natural Resource Management.

The belief and attitude statements tier down directly from these objectives. For example, an objective might be "more hiking trails." The corresponding belief question asks whether the respondent believes that providing more hiking trails is an appropriate role for the USDA Forest Service. The attitude question would then elicit input on the respondent's perception of how well the agency is doing at providing hiking trails.

The Public Lands Values were developed using approximately 200 items that, through a series of iterations using both student samples and adult samples around the United States, were reduced to 25 items. These items were designed to focus on values that people hold for the environment in general and public lands in particular. They have been tested on four National Forests in Colorado (Arapaho, Roosevelt, Pike, and San Isabel) using various traditional and non-traditional stakeholder groups. Research and testing have shown that responses to the Public Lands Values can be arranged into two categories of statements, or factors that have been labeled Socially Responsible Individual Values (SRIV) and Socially Responsible Management Values (SRMV).

The survey utilizes the objectives, beliefs, attitudes, and values statements by asking respondents to indicate their level of agreement or approval for each. Level of agreement or approval is indicated on a scale from one to five. The objectives scale items are anchored by 1=not at all important and 5=very important. The Value and Belief scale items are anchored by 1=strongly disagree and 5=strongly agree. The Attitude scale items are anchored by 1=very unfavorable and 5=very favorable.

The value scale in the VOBA survey differs from other value survey instruments in that it focuses on values associated with public lands. It is applicable at multiple spatial scales, and in addition to being used in the national VOBA survey, has been applied at the National Forest scale. Conversely, objectives may be applicable only at the regional or national scale, be location specific, or be meaningful at multiple scales. The VOBA survey objectives are applicable to the management of forests and rangelands at a broad geographic scale. Many of the objectives are also meaningful at the regional level. However, the public may have additional objectives that are specific to their home region and are not captured in the existing national survey instrument.[1]

Data Collection

The survey was implemented as a module of the National Survey on Recreation and the Environment (NSRE) with a sample size of 7,069 nationwide and 176 in Forest Service Region 3. (The number of responses in any Forest Service region is a function of the overall VOBA sampling design.) For each State the size of the sample was proportional to its population. The data were collected between late 1999 and early 2000. The NSRE is a random telephone survey administered for the Forest Service by the University of Tennessee.[2] In addition to the VOBA questions, respondents were asked about their recreational behaviors and for basic demographic information. Due to a limited amount of time available for each phone interview, each individual was asked to respond to only a portion of the full set of VOBA questions. Each respondent was asked about one fundamental objective from each of the five strategic-level objective categories. Due to this sampling design, each item in the objectives, beliefs, and attitude scales has fewer than the full 176 respondents. It is also important to note that Region 3 has a relatively low population compared to the more populous East and West Coasts. Thus, these results are an indication of a limited public's values, objectives, beliefs, and attitudes, but need to be confirmed by more intensive sampling.

The overall goal of this split sampling design was to control interview time with respondents, yet collect analytically valuable information. This not only lowers costs, but also reduces respondent burden, which should

---

[1] For more detailed information on the survey, see Shields, D., M. Martin, W. Martin, and M. Haeffle. 2002. Survey results of the American public's values, objectives, beliefs, and attitudes regarding forests and grasslands. Gen. Tech. Rep. RMRS-GTR-95. Fort Collins, CO: U.S. Department of Agriculture, Forest Service, Rocky Mountain Research Station.

[2] One drawback of a telephone survey such as the NSRE is that it will not adequately represent the views of segments of the population who do not have access to or who choose not to have telephones.

lead to fewer non-responses and therefore to a better sample quality.[3] To ensure high confidence levels, the full national survey was designed so that there was a minimum of 700 responses for each question. This design generates response numbers for each question that are adequate to support multivariate statistical analysis, and provides a high level of confidence in the results. In Region 3 the response numbers for each question ranged from 11 to 71. As a result of this smaller sample size, there is a slightly greater chance the results do not fully reflect the precise demographics of Region 3, slightly lowering the level of confidence in the results.

Finally, it is important to note that the wording of the statements within the VOBA was designed with public lands in mind. Thus some statements may raise questions concerning the appropriateness of the language for private lands. In other words, the language used may not be applicable to some types of private land use concerns, making it less appropriate to draw overarching conclusions about general land management. For example, the objective, "Developing and maintaining continuous trail systems that cross both public and private land for motorized vehicles such as snowmobiles or ATVs," is written with public land managers in mind. A similar objective, written from the perspective of private landowners might say something like, "Coordinating with public and private actors in order to support and maintain continuous trail systems that cross both public and private land for motorized vehicles." Although the wording for many of the objectives do not present this concern, it is necessary to remain aware that respondents may be thinking solely of public lands instead of both public and private lands when responding to some of the objectives.

Results for Region 3: Objectives, Beliefs, and Attitudes

Results from the Region 3 respondents to the VOBA National survey are grouped into the objectives the public in Region 3 feels are the most important, not important and moderately important. We highlight the public's level of consensus for rating each objective within these groups. We also discuss the extent to which the public feels that it is the job of the Forest Service to fulfill the objective, and examine the perception of agency performance in fulfilling these objectives. A subsequent section presents the Region 3 responses to the Public Lands Values Scale. Finally, we compare results between Region 3 and the rest of the United States.

Objectives Identified as Important

We designated a mean response of 4.00 or greater (out of a possible 5) as indicating an objective is important to the respondents in Region 3. Twelve of the original 30 objectives were thus identified as being important to the people of Region 3.

Core Important Objectives

Of the 12 important objectives, four were further singled out as "core" important objectives for the public in Region 3. These core objectives not only have means of 4.00 or higher, but also have low standard deviations (s.d. less than 1.00), indicating that the public is generally in agreement that these objectives are important.[4] The core objectives are presented in detail in table 1. For each of these four objectives we have included a histogram that compares the distribution of responses for the importance of the objective, the agency role, and customer satisfaction. In each case there is agreement that the objective is important. There is less agreement that the USDA Forest Service is the appropriate party to fulfill the objective, although the means do indicate that the majority believe this to be so. There is less agreement still about the evaluation of the agency's performance in fulfilling the objective. Two of the objectives in this group rate agency performance as favorable, two rate it as less than favorable.

Watershed protection—The VOBA objective deemed the most important by respondents in Region 3 is the conservation and protection of lands that are the source of our water resources. This objective has a mean of 4.83 and further a standard deviation of 0.76, indicating wide

---

[3] For more information on split sampling designs, see for example, Raghunathan, T.E. and Grizzle, J.E. 1995. "A Split Questionnaire Survey Design," Journal of the American Statistical Association, 90: 54-63.

[4] General agreement about the importance of these objectives is revealed with the standard deviation. The standard deviation is defined as the average amount by which scores in a distribution differ from the mean; it offers an indication of the spread of the data. For example, when looking at the importance of a given objective, the standard deviation reveals how tightly all the responses are clustered around the mean score for the stated objective. This helps to reveal if there are extreme responses or if most respondents agreed on their rating.

Table 1--Core objectives for the people of Region 3.

OBJECTIVE:	Is this an important objective for you? (1=not at all important, 5=very important)	Do you believe that fulfilling this objective is an appropriate role for the USDA Forest Service? (1=strongly disagree, 5=strongly agree)	How favorably do you view the performance of the USDA Forest Service in fulfilling this objective? (1=very unfavorably, 5=very favorably)
Conserving and protecting forests and grasslands that are the source of our water resources, such as streams, lakes, and watershed areas.	4.83 0.76[a] 29[b]	4.38 1.06 42	3.91 1.24 23
Developing volunteer programs to maintain trails and facilities on forests and grasslands (for example, trail maintenance, or campground maintenance).	4.39 0.78 23	4.17 1.07 29	3.55 1.28 20
Developing volunteer programs to improve forests and grasslands (for example, tree planting, or improving water quality).	4.53 0.84 36	4.46 1.10 28	2.83 1.27 23
Informing the public on the economic value received by developing our natural resources.	4.16 0.94 25	4.08 1.32 24	2.69 1.41 26

[a] Standard deviation
[b] Sample size for each item (n). The sample sizes for each item are less than the full 176 sample since each respondent was asked only a portion of the 115 VOBA questions due to time limitations.

agreement about the importance of this objective. Protecting watersheds is viewed as an appropriate role for the USDA Forest Service (mean=4.38), but with somewhat less consensus (s.d.=1.06). Agency performance in fulfilling this objective is rated as somewhat favorable, but with still less agreement (mean=3.91, s.d.=1.24). This decreasing consensus from the importance of the objective to the evaluation of agency performance can be seen in figure 2 which shows the distribution of responses or scores.

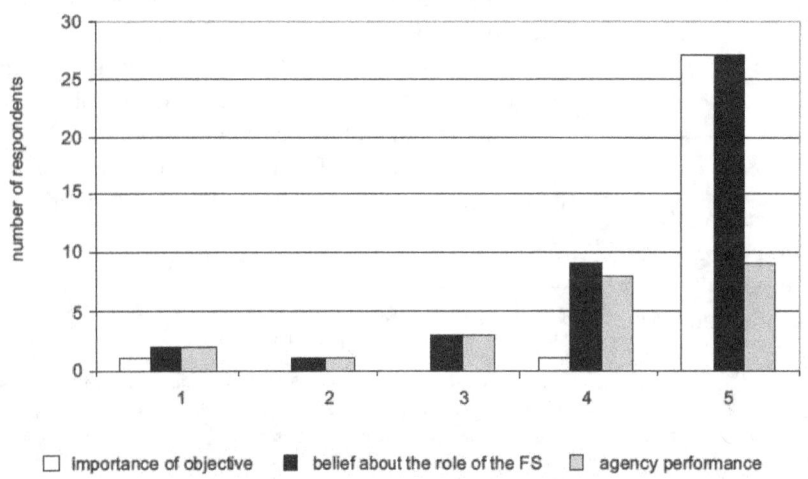

Figure 2—Distribution of Objective, Belief and Attitude scores for: Conserving and protecting forests and grasslands that are the source of our water sources.

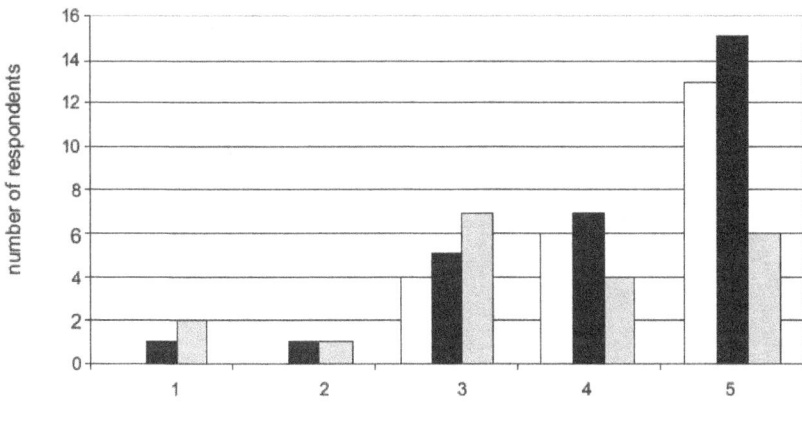

Figure 3—Distribution of Objective, Belief and Attitude scores for: Developing volunteer programs to maintain trails and facilities on forests and grasslands.

☐ importance of objective   ■ belief about the role of the FS   ☐ agency performance

Volunteer Programs—Two types of volunteer programs are core objectives for the residents of Region 3. Programs to maintain facilities such as trails and campgrounds are widely agreed to be important (mean=4.39, s.d.=0.78). Providing such programs is also seen by most of the respondents in the Region as an appropriate role for the Forest Service, but with somewhat less agreement (mean=4.17, s.d.=1.07). While the agency is viewed as doing a somewhat favorable job, there is even less agreement (mean=3.55, s.d. =1.28) about this evaluation, as can be seen in the distribution of responses shown in figure 3.

Volunteer programs that target the health of forests and grasslands, such as tree planting are also important to most residents of Region 3 (mean=4.53, s.d.=0.84). Providing such programs is seen as an appropriate role

for the agency but with a similar decline in the level of agreement (mean=4.46, s.d.=1.10). Agency performance is slightly unfavorable (mean=2.83). The level of consensus for this evaluation is not high (s.d.=1.27). Figure 4 shows the responses to this objective, and illustrates the decreasing consensus from the importance of the objective to the evaluation of agency performance.

Information on Economic Benefits—The final core objective for Region 3 residents is the provision of information to the public about the economic value received from the development of natural resources (mean=4.16, s.d.=0.94). Overall the respondents in Region 3 feel that providing such information is an important role for the agency, although there is little agreement with this general statement (mean=4.08, s.d.=1.32). Agency performance is rated as somewhat unfavorable (mean=2.69),

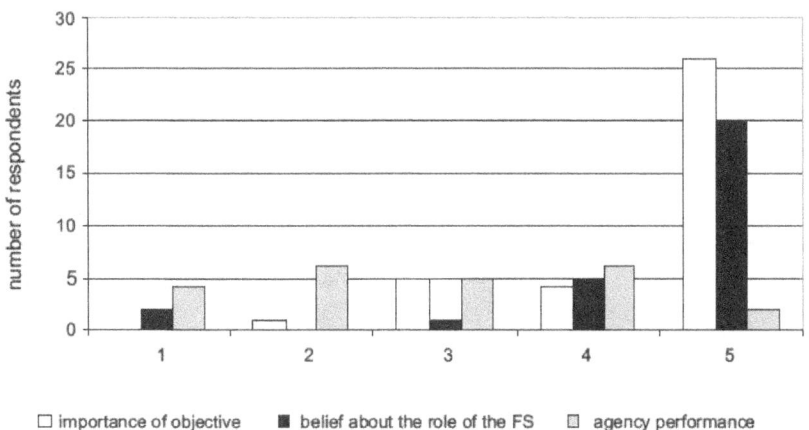

Figure 4—Distribution of Objective, Belief and Attitude scores for: Developing volunteer programs to improve forests and grasslands (for example, planting trees or improving water quality).

☐ importance of objective   ■ belief about the role of the FS   ☐ agency performance

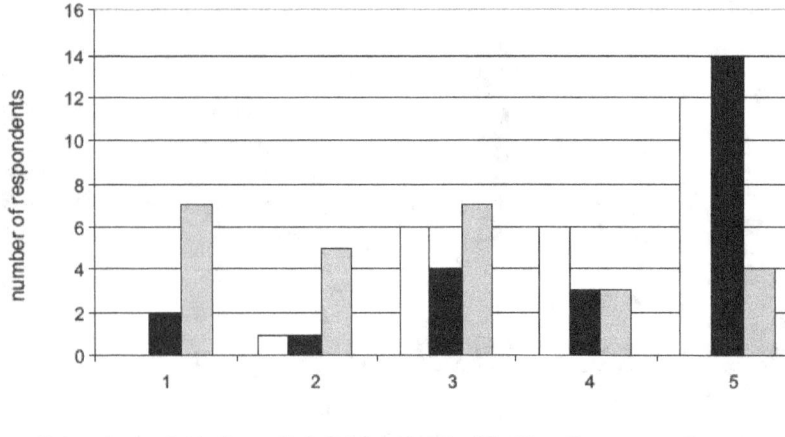

Figure 5—Distribution of Objective, Belief and Attitude scores for: Informing the public on the economic value received by developing natural resources.

☐ importance of objective ■ belief about the role of the FS ☐ agency performance

but this view is also not universal, as indicated by the standard deviation of 1.41. The distribution of responses for this objective is shown in figure 5.

Other Important Objectives

Table 2 shows the results for the other eight objectives that respondents in Region 3 identified as important. These issues, while viewed as important based on means over 4.00, do not enjoy as wide agreement as the core issues. These means have higher standard deviations, indicating more diverse responses from the public. The objectives in table 2 are ordered from those with the lowest standard deviation (higher consensus) to those with higher standard deviations (less consensus). As a result, some objectives identified as relatively more important fall lower in the table than objectives identified as relatively less important. Each of these objectives will be discussed briefly.

Although Region 3 residents report that the development of a national policy to guide resource development on public lands is an important objective (mean=4.31), agreement on this assessment is not universal (s.d.=1.01). It is generally believed by residents in Region 3 that the Forest Service would be within its bounds to provide such national direction (mean=4.30, s.d.=0.92). Assessment of the agency's performance is neutral and exhibits a lack of consensus (mean=3.00, s.d.=1.15).

Overall, the residents of Region 3 report that allowing for diverse uses of forests and grasslands is an important objective, although the level of consensus is slightly low (mean=4.12, s.d.=1.07). Region 3 residents believe that fulfilling this objective is an appropriate role for the USDA Forest Service, but again with somewhat low

agreement (mean=4.00, s.d.=1.15). Agency performance in providing for diverse uses is determined by Region 3 respondents to be somewhat favorable (mean=3.84, s.d. =1.00).

While protecting ecosystems and wildlife habitat is an important objective for most respondents in Region 3, there is some lack of agreement (mean=4.51, s.d.=1.08). Respondents do believe that the Forest Service should be fulfilling this objective (mean=4.47, s.d.=1.01), and agency performance is evaluated as somewhat favorable, but with a great deal of disagreement (mean=3.45, s.d.=1.41).

Law enforcement on public lands is important to Region 3 residents, although, again, there is a lack of agreement (mean=4.0, s.d.=1.08). Overall, respondents in Region 3 believe that increasing law enforcement is a somewhat appropriate role for the USDA Forest Service, but there is considerable disagreement in the precise rating (mean=3.59, s.d.=1.26). Finally, agency performance is viewed as somewhat favorable, although there is a great deal of variation concerning this evaluation (mean=3.82, s.d.=1.33).

Restricting mineral development on forests and grasslands is important to Region 3 residents (mean=4.09). Additionally, while the level of agreement is not high for this issue, it also is not as low as one might expect for such a controversial objective (s.d. =1.11). Respondents believe that the USDA Forest Service is an appropriate agency to fulfill this objective, but here we see considerable disagreement (mean=3.77, s.d.=1.51). The evaluation of the job the agency is doing in fulfilling this objective is not favorable (mean=2.45, s.d.=1.15).

Table 2--Objectives that Region 3 respondents view as important.

OBJECTIVE:	Is this an important objective for you? *(1=not at all important, 5=very important)*	Do you believe that fulfilling this objective is an appropriate role for the USDA Forest Service? *(1=strongly disagree, 5=strongly agree)*	How favorably do you view the performance of the USDA Forest Service in fulfilling this objective? *(1=very unfavorably, 5=very favorably)*
Developing a national policy that guides natural resource development of all kinds (for example, specifies levels of extraction, and regulates environmental impacts).	4.31 *1.01*[a] 36[b]	4.30 *0.92* 20	3.00 *1.13* 15
Allowing for diverse uses of forests and grasslands such as grazing, recreation, and wildlife habitat.	4.12 *1.07* 26	4.00 *1.15* 25	3.84 *1.00* 31
Protecting ecosystems and wildlife habitats.	4.51 *1.08* 41	4.47 *1.01* 30	3.45 *1.41* 31
Increasing law enforcement efforts by public land agencies on public lands.	4.00 *1.08* 18	3.59 *1.26* 22	3.82 *1.33* 17
Restricting mineral development on forests and grasslands.	4.09 *1.11* 22	3.77 *1.51* 22	2.45 *1.15* 29
Preserving the ability to have a "wilderness experience" on forests and grasslands.	4.00 *1.18* 27	4.22 *1.12* 27	4.06 *0.90* 33
Informing the public about recreation concerns on forests and grasslands such as safety, trail etiquette, and respect for wildlife).	4.39 *1.20* 23	4.32 *0.99* 22	3.44 *1.31* 27
Making management decisions concerning the use of forests and grasslands at the local level rather than at the national level.	4.05 *1.39* 19	4.17 *0.98* 23	3.06 *1.48* 16

[a] Standard deviation
[b] Sample size for each item (n). The sample sizes for each item are less than the full 176 sample since each respondent was asked only a portion of the 115 VOBA questions due to time limitations.

Interpretation of this evaluation is difficult since one who feels this is an important objective will have different criteria for agency performance than does one who feels that it is not an important objective.

Preserving the ability to have a "wilderness experience" on forests and grasslands is viewed by Region 3 respondents as important (mean=4.00), but this objective does not enjoy a great deal of consensus (s.d.=1.18). Providing such experiences is seen as an appropriate role for the Forest Service, but again there is little agreement concerning this assessment (mean=4.22, s.d.=1.12). Agency performance is rated as favorable, and the level of agreement here is high (mean=4.06, s.d.=0.90).

Generally speaking, the residents of Region 3 feel that providing information to the public about recreation concerns such as trail etiquette and safety is an important objective (mean=4.39, s.d.=1.20). These respondents also are in relative agreement that it is important for the Forest Service to be providing such information (mean=4.32, s.d.=0.99). Agency performance is rated as favorable, although there is a low level of consensus for this assessment (mean=3.44, s.d.=1.31).

Finally, the respondents in Region 3 feel that making public land management decisions at the local level is an important objective (mean=4.05). Again, there is disagreement with this assessment, as indicated by the standard deviation of 1.39. Region 3 residents also believe it is appropriate that the Forest Service confine decisions to the local level, and here the level of agreement is high (mean=4.17, s.d.=0.98). Agency performance is only slightly favorable, but this rating exhibits very little consensus (mean=3.06, s.d.=1.48).

Objectives Identified as Not Important

Five objectives in the VOBA questionnaire are not important to the majority of respondents in Region 3. These objectives have a mean importance rating of less than 3.00 (3.00 is the midpoint of the scale, indicating a neutral position). While the means for these objectives indicate that most respondents did not feel that they were important, these objectives also exhibit high standard deviations, indicating that there are supporters as well. This is not surprising since these objectives were included in the VOBA survey based upon the input of focus groups. Some focus groups, who are representative of elements within society, revealed strong preferences for these objectives. Therefore, it is likely these same stakeholder groups showed support for these objectives. In other words, while the general public does not feel these objectives are important, there is a vocal minority that does. These less important objectives are presented in table 3.

Motorized recreation is often considered a controversial use of public lands. Results from Region 3 support this assertion. The respondents of Region 3, on the whole, do not find the provision of access for motorized vehicles to be very important, but there is wide disagreement about this (mean=2.95, s.d.=1.53). Most respondents do not believe that the Forest Service is the appropriate agency to provide motorized access, although again there are some respondents who disagree (mean-=2.29, s.d.=1.51). Agency performance is not favorable, but again, there is a great deal of disagreement about this evaluation (mean=2.40, s.d.=1.55). Figure 6 shows the distribution of scores.

Many uses of public lands require a permit. Easing the permitting process is not regarded as an important objective for Region 3 residents, but as with all the objectives in this group, the level of agreement about this assessment is low (mean=2.86, s.d.=1.35). Region 3 residents also generally do not feel that it is the role of the USDA Forest Service to relax the permit procedures (mean=2.76, s.d.=1.20). As with other objectives that

Table 3--Objectives that Region 3 respondents do not view as important.

OBJECTIVE:	Is this an important objective for you? *(1=not at all important, 5=very important)*	Do you believe that fulfilling this objective is an appropriate role for the USDA Forest Service? *(1=strongly disagree, 5=strongly agree)*	How favorably do you view the performance of the USDA Forest Service in fulfilling this objective? *(1=very unfavorably, 5=very favorably)*
Expanding access for motorized off-highway vehicles on forests and grasslands (for example, snowmobiling or 4-wheel driving).	2.95 *1.53[a]* 22[b]	2.29 *1.51* 31	2.40 *1.55* 15
Making the permitting process easier for some established uses of forests and grasslands such as grazing, logging, mining, and commercial recreation.	2.86 *1.35* 21	2.76 *1.20* 17	3.20 *1.42* 15
Expanding commercial recreation on forests and grasslands (for example, ski areas, guide services and outfitters).	2.85 *1.39* 20	2.94 *1.41* 32	3.70 *0.92* 20
Developing and maintaining continuous trail systems that cross both public and private land for motorized vehicles such as snowmobiles and ATV's.	2.82 *1.53* 22	3.21 *1.69* 28	3.04 *1.40* 24
Developing new paved roads on forests and grasslands for access for cars and recreational vehicles.	2.42 *1.46* 19	2.37 *1.47* 27	3.04 *1.19* 23

[a] Standard deviation
[b] Sample size for each item (n). The sample sizes for each item are less than the full 176 sample since each respondent was asked only a portion of the 115 VOBA questions due to time limitations.

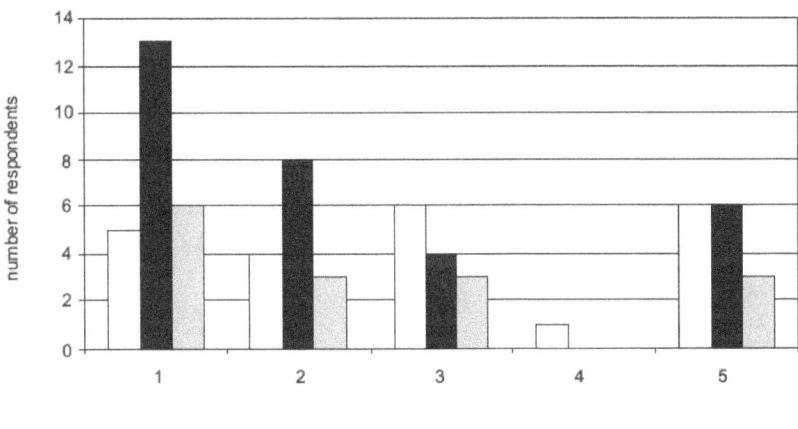

Figure 6—Distribution of Objective, Belief and Attitude scores for: Expanding access for motorized off-highway vehicles on forests and grasslands.

□ importance of objective ■ belief about the role of the FS □ agency performance

are not seen as falling within the purview of the agency, interpretation of the agency's performance can be inconclusive. Here, respondents in Region 3 rate agency performance as somewhat favorable (mean=3.20), with the usual dissent (s.d.=1.42). It should be noted that the criteria used for this evaluation will differ depending on whether a respondent finds the objective important or feels that it is the role of the agency to fulfill it. Figure 7 shows the distribution and the diversity in responses for this objective.

Expanding commercial recreation on forests and grasslands is not important to the majority of respondents in Region 3, but this is not a universal evaluation (mean=2.85, s.d.=1.39). Respondents do not feel that implementing expanded commercial recreation is an appropriate role for the agency (mean=2.94, s.d.=1.41). Agency performance is rated as favorable, and there is relative agreement about this evaluation (mean=3.70,

s.d.=0.92). See figure 8 for the distribution of Region 3 responses for this objective.

Developing and maintaining a continuous system of trails (crossing public and private lands) for motorized access is not viewed by most Region 3 residents as an important objective (mean=2.82). However, as with other objectives in this group, the standard deviation (1.53) reveals there are those who do view it as important. Providing such a trail system is seen as an appropriate role for the USDA Forest Service, but this belief does not have wide agreement (mean=3.21, s.d.=1.69). Agency performance is viewed as slightly favorable, but there is a low level of agreement about this assessment (mean=3.04, s.d.=1.40). Figure 9 shows the high level of variation in these responses.

Motorized access often requires paved roads. In spite of this, expanding the number of paved roads on forests and grasslands is not important to the residents

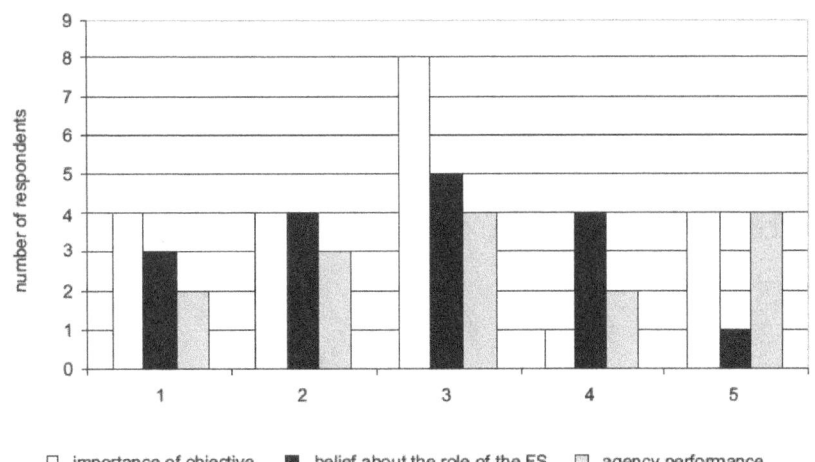

Figure 7—Distribution of Objective, Belief and Attitude scores for: Making the permitting process easier for some established uses of forests and grasslands.

□ importance of objective ■ belief about the role of the FS □ agency performance

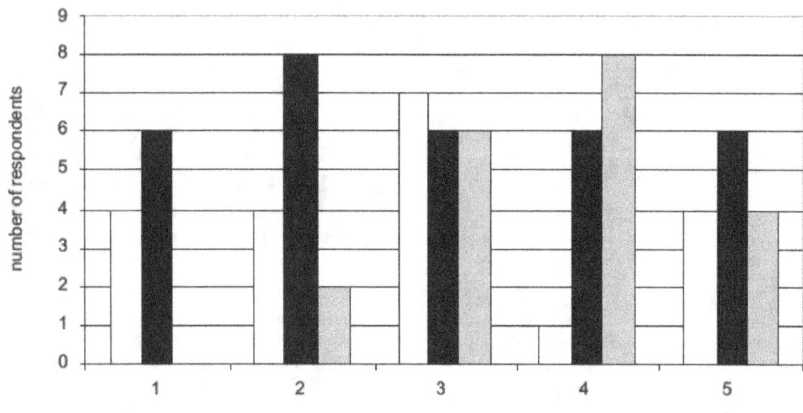

Figure 8—Distribution of Objective, Belief and Attitude scores for: Expanding commercial recreation on forests and grasslands.

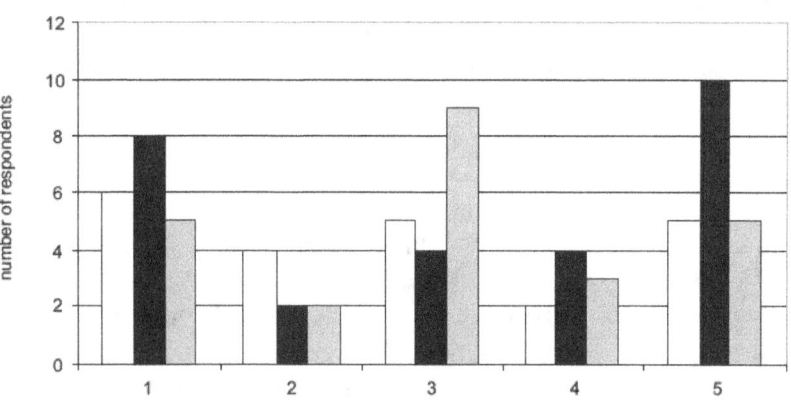

Figure 9—Distribution of Objective, Belief and Attitude scores for: Developing and maintaining continuous trail systems for motorized vehicles.

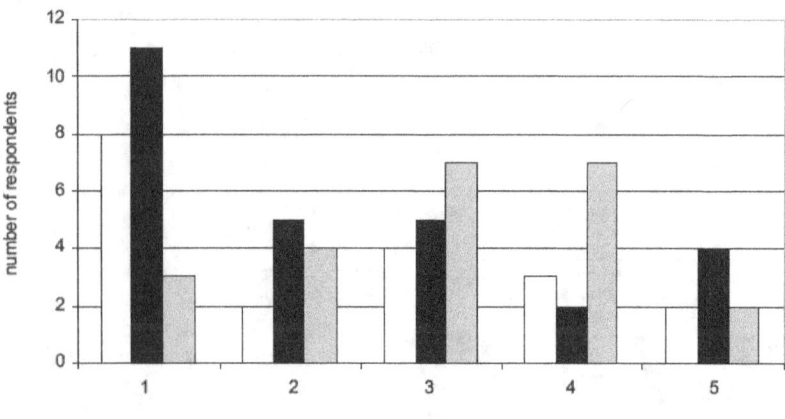

Figure 10—Distribution of Objective, Belief and Attitude scores for: Developing new paved roads on forests and grasslands for access for cars and recreational vehicles.

of Region 3 (mean=2.42). Again, not all agree with this assessment (s.d.=1.46). Expanding paved roads is not viewed as an appropriate role for the Forest Service by most respondents in Region 3 (mean=2.37, s.d.=1.47). The Forest Service is seen by many as doing a relatively favorable job of expanding roads (mean=3.04, s.d.=1.19). Figure 10 shows the distribution of responses for this objective.

Objectives Identified as Moderately Important

Table 4 presents the objectives that the people of Region 3 feel are somewhat important, or those for which they are more neutral. All of these moderately important objectives have means between 3.00 and 4.00. As with the less important objectives, they all also have higher standard deviations, indicating that while most people do not feel strongly about them, a few do. Again, given how the set of objectives was developed, it is not surprising to find a variety of responses. Results for this group of objectives have been organized in table 4 to facilitate a discussion of related issues. For example, objectives that deal either directly or indirectly with resource extraction are grouped together. Within these groupings, the objectives are organized in order of decreasing importance (objectives with higher means first, then those with lower means).

Resource Extraction and Use

The preservation of natural resources of forests and grasslands through policies that end timber harvesting and mining is of moderate importance to the people of Region 3 (mean=3.91), although there is some disagreement as can be seen in the standard deviation (1.38). The residents of Region 3 do feel that enacting such policies is an appropriate role for the Forest Service (mean=4.06, s.d.=1.18) and that the agency is doing an adequate job (mean=3.42, s.d.=1.36), although there is also some disagreement about both of these evaluations.

Restricting timber harvest and grazing is also seen by Region 3 residents as moderately important, but there is great variety in responses to this objective (mean=3.88, s.d.=1.62). This objective, while similar to the previous one, is worded without any justification of such a policy, which may be the source of the decrease in consensus. Respondents in Region 3 may see restrictions on extractive uses of forests and grasslands as justified when it is made clear that the purpose is the preservation of natural resources (although there is still a good deal of

disagreement about this). Region 3 residents see the implementation of such restrictions as a somewhat appropriate role for the USDA Forest Service (mean=3.74), but the high standard deviation reveals a great deal of disagreement about this (1.44). Agency performance is slightly unfavorable (mean=2.96, s.d.=1.26).

The forests and grasslands in Region 3 have a number of traditional cultural uses by Native Americans and Native Hispanics. Preserving these cultural uses is seen by residents in the Region as a somewhat important objective (mean=3.81). This opinion is not shared by all within the Region, as can be seen in the large standard deviation (1.30). Providing access for such uses is believed to be an appropriate role for the Forests Service, but again, this belief is not universal (mean=3.65, s.d.=1.50). Agency performance is rated favorably according to Region 3 respondents, and with wide agreement (mean=3.60, s.d.=0.91).

Wilderness designation is often a subject on which there is little agreement. Region 3 is no exception. While generally the residents of the Region do feel that designation of more wilderness is important (mean=3.80), there are a variety of responses for this objective (s.d.=1.44). Perhaps reflecting knowledge about the actual process by which wilderness is designated, Region 3 residents do not believe that such designation is the role of the USDA Forest Service (mean=2.94). However, this belief is not widely shared (s.d.=1.68). Agency performance is slightly unfavorable, although, again, this is not a universally held evaluation (mean=2.95, s.d.=1.24).

Public land management conflicts often arise due to differing priorities. Communities which are adjacent to public lands often see these lands as the source of their livelihood, while those more distant prefer that other uses be emphasized. The residents in Region 3 see the provision of resources to dependent communities as a somewhat important objective (mean=3.54). But, as we often see with this group of objectives, the level of agreement is very low (s.d.=1.65). Providing resources to dependent communities is seen as a slightly appropriate role for the USDA Forest Service, yet again, there is disagreement with this assessment (mean=3.05, s.d.=1.33). Agency performance is somewhat favorable (mean=3.28, s.d.=1.24).

Public Input and Information

Collaborative management is being applied more and more in Federal land management. The Region 3 respondents feel that encouraging such collaboration (table 4) is a moderately important objective (mean=3.90),

Table 4--Objectives of moderate importance for Region 3.

OBJECTIVE:		Is this an important objective for you? *(1=not at all important, 5=very important)*	Do you believe that fulfilling this objective is an appropriate role for the USDA Forest Service? *(1=strongly disagree, 5=strongly agree)*	How favorably do you view the performance of the USDA Forest Service in fulfilling this objective? *(1=very unfavorably, 5=very favorably)*
Resource Extraction and Use	Preserving the natural resources of forests and grasslands through such policies as no timber harvesting or no mining.	3.91 *1.38*[a] 23[b]	4.06 *1.18* 31	3.42 *1.36* 26
	Restricting timber harvesting and grazing on forests and grasslands.	3.88 *1.62* 24	3.74 *1.44* 35	2.96 *1.26* 23
	Preserving the cultural uses of forests and grasslands by Native Americans and Native Hispanics[#] such as firewood gathering, herb/berry/ plant gathering, and ceremonial access.	3.81 *1.30* 31	3.65 *1.50* 23	3.60 *0.91* 25
	Designating more wilderness areas on public land that stops access for development and motorized uses.	3.80 *1.44* 41	2.94 *1.68* 17	2.95 *1.24* 21
	Providing natural resources from forests and grasslands to support communities dependent on grazing, mining, or timber harvesting.	3.54 *1.65* 26	3.05 *1.33* 22	3.28 *1.24* 25
Public Input & Information	Encouraging collaboration between groups in order to share information concerning uses of forests and grasslands.	3.90 *1.17* 20	4.63 *0.71* 24	3.81 *1.08* 21
	Informing the public on the potential environmental impacts of all uses associated with forests and grasslands.	3.90 *1.48* 21	4.32 *0.99* 25	3.57 *1.38* 23
	Using public advisory committees to advise on public land management issues.	3.57 *1.31* 23	3.89 *1.23* 18	2.82 *1.25* 11
Recreation	Designating some existing recreation trails for specific uses (for example, creating separate trails for snowmobiling and cross-country skiing, or for mountain biking and horseback riding).	3.67 *1.33* 27	3.57 *1.29* 21	3.17 *0.99* 18
	Developing and maintaining continuous trail systems that cross both public and private land for non-motorized recreation such as hiking or cross-country skiing.	3.67 *1.35* 15	4.36 *1.19* 25	3.50 *1.19* 22
	Paying an entry fee that goes to support public land.	3.44 *1.34* 18	3.41 *1.40* 22	3.45 *1.15* 20
Land Acquisition	Allowing public land managers to trade public lands for private lands (for example, to eliminate private property within public land boundaries, or to acquire unique areas of land).	3.40 *1.64* 15	3.40 *1.10* 20	2.95 *1.17* 22
	Increasing the total number of acres in the public land system.	3.38 *1.32* 29	3.86 *1.24* 21	3.38 *1.45* 13

[a] Standard deviation

[b] Sample size for each item (n). The sample sizes for each item are less than the full 176 sample since each respondent was asked only a portion of the 115 VOBA questions due to time limitations.

[#] The term "Native Hispanic" was used in the survey to differentiate Hispanics born in the US from those who moved to the US This term was changed to "traditional groups" in the 2003 survey

although there is some disagreement about this assessment (s.d.=1.17). These respondents agree that the Forest Service should be encouraging collaboration (mean=4.63, s.d.=0.71), and the agency is generally perceived as performing adequately in fulfilling this objective (mean=3.81, s.d.=1.08).

Dissatisfaction over management of public lands often stems from the environmental impacts that occur with certain uses. Informing the public on the environmental impacts associated with uses of forests and grasslands is moderately important to the majority of respondents in Region 3. However there is also a great deal of dissent from this opinion (mean=3.90, s.d.=1.48). Region 3 residents agree that providing the public with this information is an appropriate role for the USDA Forest Service (mean=4.32, s.d.=0.99). The Forest Service is seen as doing a good job providing this information, although the level of agreement is low for this evaluation (mean=3.57, s.d.=1.38).

Public input into forest and grassland management decisions is always important to some stakeholders. The form for this input can influence how participation takes place, and how people feel about the process. In the same spirit as collaboration, many people have advocated using public advisory committees to inform land management decision makers and to provide input into management decisions. Generally speaking, the people of Region 3 find the use of such committees to be somewhat important, but there a variety of opinions on this issue (mean=3.57, s.d.=1.31). Using advisory committees is believed by Region 3 residents to be an appropriate role for the agency, although there is disagreement about this too (mean=3.89, s.d.=1.23). Finally, the performance of the USDA Forest Service is viewed as slightly unfavorable (mean=2.82, s.d.=1.25).

Recreation

Conflicts between incompatible recreation uses are often an issue on public lands, including those in the National Forest System. One solution would be to designate some trails for specific uses, for example separate trails for cross-country skiing and snowmobiling. Designating such specific use trails is seen as somewhat important to the Region 3 respondents, although there is some disagreement with this evaluation (mean=3.67, s.d.=1.33). Creating such designations for trails is believed by Region 3 residents to be an appropriate role for the Forest Service (mean=3.57). However, this belief is not shared by all respondents (s.d.=1.29). Most respondents agree

that agency performance is slightly favorable for this objective (mean=3.17, s.d.=0.99).

Developing and maintaining a continuous trail system that crosses both private and public land for non-motorized recreation is a somewhat important objective for the residents of Region 3 (mean=3.67). That opinion is not shared by all respondents, as can be seen in the high standard deviation (1.35). It is an interesting comparison to note that the residents of Region 3 do not find the development of a similar trail system for motorized recreation to be important (see table 3 above). The USDA Forest Service is seen as an appropriate agency to fulfill this objective, although there is some dissention with this assessment (mean=4.36, s.d.=1.19). Agency performance is evaluated as favorable (mean=3.50, s.d.=1.19).

Many public land recreation opportunities are available only to fee-paying users. This has been a source of some controversy in recent years. Paying an entry fee that goes to support public land is an objective that residents in Region 3 feel is somewhat important (mean=3.44). However, the high standard deviation reveals that this objective has very little consensus (1.34). Although not everyone agrees, generally speaking, implementing an entry fee is believed to be an appropriate role for the agency (mean=3.41, s.d.=1.40). The USDA Forest Service is seen as doing a favorable job (mean=3.45, s.d.=1.15).

Land Acquisition

Allowing public land managers to trade public lands for private lands is a somewhat important objective for Region 3 residents, but this objective is far from universally supported (mean=3.40, s.d.=1.64). The USDA Forest Service is viewed as the appropriate agency to fulfill this objective (mean=3.40), although again there is not universal agreement (s.d.=1.10). Agency performance is not viewed favorably, with a mean of 2.95 and standard deviation of 1.17.

A similar objective to trading public lands for private is the objective of increasing the total acreage in the public lands system. The people of Region 3 find this to be a somewhat important objective, but as with the other objectives in this group, there is not a great deal of consensus for this evaluation (mean=3.38, s.d.=1.32). Increasing the total acreage in the public land system is seen as an appropriate role for the Forest Service, but again there is a lack of consensus (mean=3.86, s.d.=1.24). Generally Region 3 respondents view agency performance as favorable, but there are diverse opinions on this issue (mean 3.38, s.d.=1.45).

Results for Region 3: Public Lands Values_____

Previous research using the Public Lands Values Scale has shown that these items consistently fall into two categories. The first, containing items that deal with individual actions or values, we have labeled as Socially Responsible Individual Values (tables 5 and 6). For the Socially Responsible Individual Values, a higher mean indicates a higher level of environmental orientation. The second category contains items that deal with how public lands should be managed. These are called the Socially Responsible Management Values (table 7). The Socially Responsible Management Values statements are worded so that a higher value indicates that relatively more importance is placed upon human uses of, or commodity production from, forests and grasslands.

Socially Responsible Individual Values

The responses to the Socially Responsible Individual Values will be further broken into two groups; those for which there is a high degree of consensus and those for which the level of agreement is lower (based upon the standard deviation). Most of the means for the values indicate an environmental orientation in the people of Region 3, but for many of the values statements, the standard deviation indicates that the level of agreement is low.

Socially Responsible Individual Values with a High Degree of Consensus

When those Socially Responsible Individual Values for which there is a higher degree of agreement (standard deviation of 1.00 or less) are placed in order of increasing standard deviation, the order of agreement is not analogously decreasing (table 5). Nonetheless, the values statements with higher means (indicating a more environmental value orientation) are also those with higher levels of consensus.

Socially Responsible Individual Values with a Low Degree of Consensus

Table 6 shows the values statements that have lower consensus among the respondents. These again nearly always exhibit the characteristic that higher levels of environmental orientation also correspond to higher consensus (even among these values with low consensus).

Figure 11 shows the distribution of responses to the statement "I would be willing to pay $5 more each time I use public lands for recreational purposes." While many respondents agree with this statement (mean=3.22), the high standard deviation indicates that there is a great deal of disagreement (s.d.=1.52). Examination of figure 11 reveals there are nearly as many respondents who do not agree with the statement, as there are those that do agree. Additionally, there are a great number of respondents who are at best neutral. Since fees are often a reality in order to provide such recreation opportunities, it is important to be aware that while most support them, such policies will also most likely meet with considerable resistance.

Table 5--Socially responsible individual public lands values for Region 3 with a high level of agreement among respondents.

Values *(1=strongly disagree. 5=strongly agree)*	Mean
I am glad there are national forests even if I never get to see them.	4.69 *0.78*[a] 52[b]
Donating time or money to worthy causes is important to me.	4.17 *0.99* 53
Manufacturers should be encouraged to use recycled materials in their manufacturing and processing operations.	4.63 *1.00* 40

[a] Standard deviation
[b] Sample size for each item (n). The sample sizes for each item are less than the full 176 sample since each respondent was asked only a portion of the 115 VOBA questions due to time limitations.

Table 6--Socially responsible individual public lands values for Region 3 with a low level of agreement among respondents.

Values *(1=strongly disagree, 5=strongly agree)*	Mean
Future generations should be just as important as the current one in the decisions about public lands.	4.52 *1.03*[a] 61[b]
I am willing to make personal sacrifices for the sake of slowing down pollution.	4.15 *1.10* 40
Consumers should be interested in the environmental consequences of the products they purchase.	4.15 *1.14* 39
Forests have a right to exist for their own sake, regardless of human concerns and uses.	4.17 *1.15* 42
People can think public lands are valuable even if they never go there themselves.	4.31 *1.17* 51
I am willing to stop buying products from companies that pollute the environment even though it might be inconvenient.	3.98 *1.26* 43
People should be more concerned about how our public lands are used.	4.16 *1.28* 37
The whole pollution issue has never upset me too much since I feel it's somewhat overrated. [c]	3.84 *1.36* 45
I have often thought that if we could just get by with a little less there would be more left for future generations.	3.80 *1.38* 49
People should urge their friends to limit their use of products made from scarce resources.	3.63 *1.40* 43
Natural resources should be preserved even if people must do without some products.	3.71 *1.41* 58
Wildlife, plants, and humans have equal rights to live and grow.	3.90 *1.49* 49
I would be willing to pay five dollars more each time I use public lands for recreational purposes.	3.22 *1.52* 59
I would be willing to sign a petition for an environmental cause.	3.45 *1.60* 47

[a] Standard deviation
[b] Sample size for each item (n). The sample sizes for each item are less than the full 176 sample since each respondent was asked only a portion of the 115 VOBA questions due to time limitations.
[c] This value statement has been reverse scored to make the responses consistent with the other statements. For a more complete discussion of reverse scoring, please refer to the appendix.

Table 7--Socially responsible management public lands values for Region 3.

Values *(1=strongly disagree. 5=strongly agree)*	Mean
The Federal government should subsidize the development and leasing of public lands to companies.	1.79 *1.18*[a] *47*[b]
The primary use of forests should be for products that are useful to humans.	2.37 *1.22* *71*
I think that the public land managers are doing an adequate job of protecting natural resources from being overused.	3.04 *1.38* *47*
The most important role for the public lands is providing jobs and income for local people.	2.53 *1.40* *68*
The decision to develop resources should be based mostly on economic grounds.	2.83 *1.40* *53*
The government has better places to spend money than devoting resources to a strong conservation program.	2.40 *1.46* *58*
We should actively harvest more trees to meet the needs of a much larger human population.	2.58 *1.47* *52*
The main reason for maintaining resources today is so we can use them in the future if we need to.	3.43 *1.51* *56*

[a] Standard deviation
[b] Sample size for each item (n). The sample sizes for each item are less than the full 176 sample since each respondent was asked only a portion of the 115 VOBA questions due to time limitations.

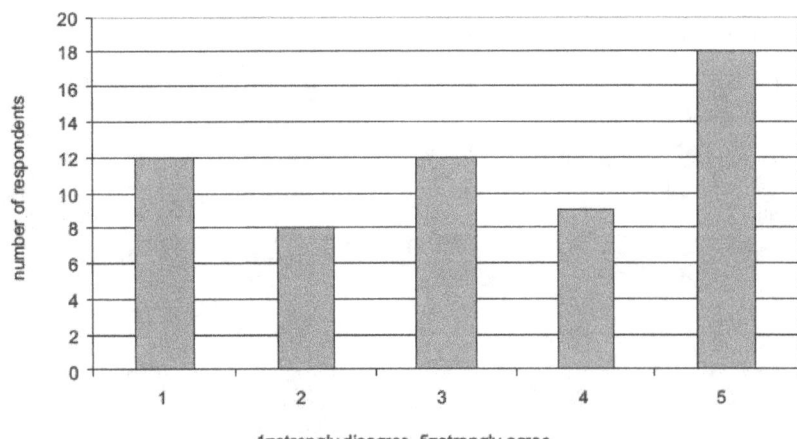

Figure 11—Distribution of responses to: "I would be willing to pay five dollars more each time I used public lands for recreational purposes."

USDA Forest Service RMRS-GTR-156. 2005.

Socially Responsible Management Values

The results for the Socially Responsible Management Values (table 7) have not been separated by level of consensus, as none of them show a high level of consensus. They are presented in the table in order of decreasing consensus. As the previous section demonstrates, most people believe in protecting the environment. Disagreement arises about the appropriate methods to achieve such protection. The differences in responses to this set of values are the basis for the disagreement we see in some of the objectives. Histograms are presented for the distribution of responses for each of the Socially Responsible Management Values (figures 12 through 19), but only the first two are discussed because of their direct relevance to land management and customer satisfaction.

It is interesting to note the low level of agreement with the statement "The Federal government should subsidize the development and leasing of public lands to companies." Also of interest is the relatively high consensus on this opinion among responses from the public in Region 3. This response is, while not statistically significant, different from the rest of the United States, where there is a higher level of agreement and a lower level of consensus. Figure 12 shows the distribution of responses to this statement.

There is wide disagreement about the statement "I think the public land managers are doing an adequate job of protecting natural resources from being over used" (figure 13). This value statement may in part explain the overall low means for attitudes about agency performance on specific issues. Here we see that the overall assessment of public land managers is neutral. Generally people neither agree nor disagree with the statement (mean=3.04). However, when asked about the performance of a specific agency (the USDA Forest Service) in fulfilling a specific objective, most people have stronger opinions, and these have been revealed in the attitude statements discussed in previous sections.

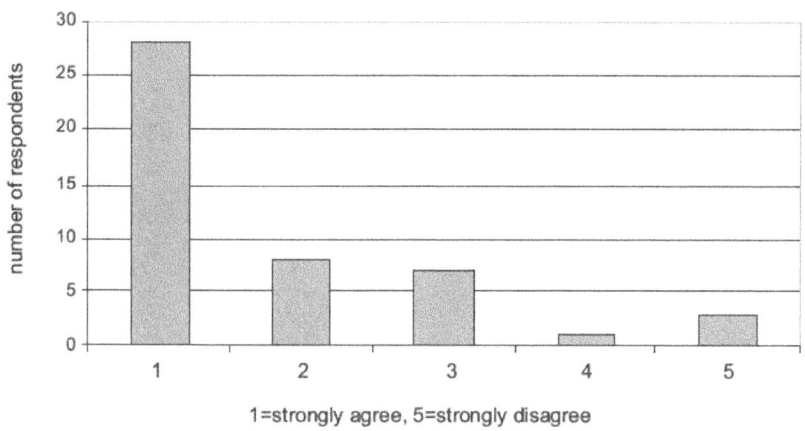

Figure 12—Distribution of responses to: "The Federal government should subsidize the development and leasing of public lands to companies."

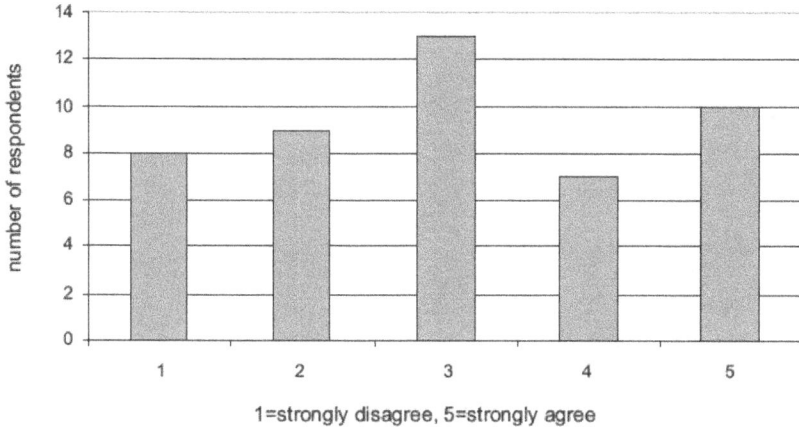

Figure 13—Distribution of responses to: "I think that the public land managers are doing an adequate job of protecting natural resources from being overused."

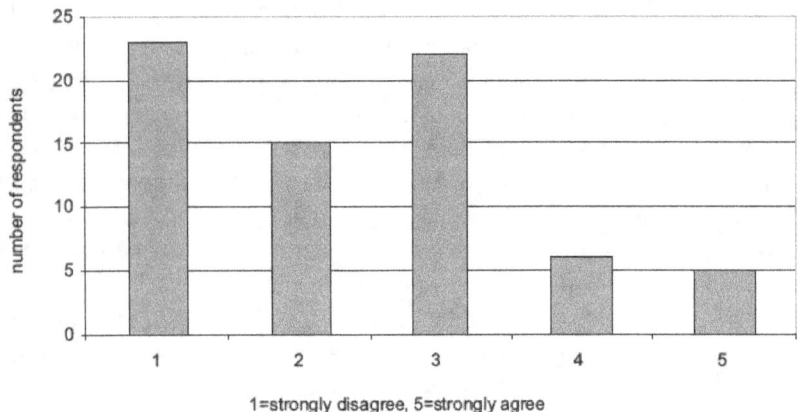

Figure 14—Distribution of responses to: "I think that the primary use of forests should be for products that are useful to humans."

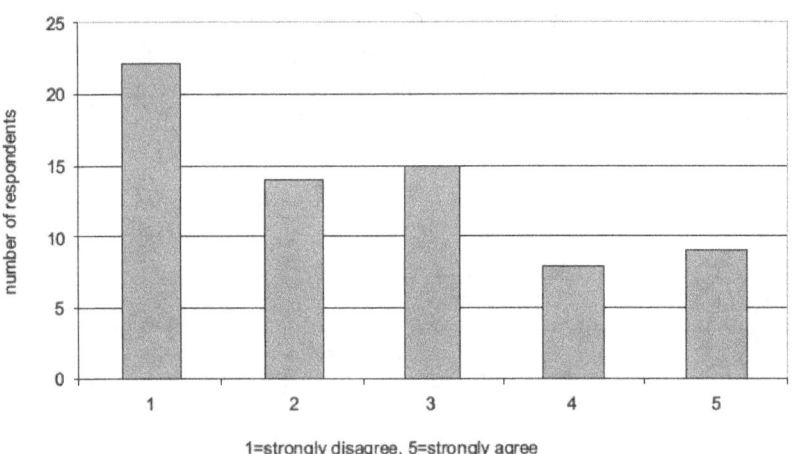

Figure 15—Distribution of responses to: "The most important role for the public lands is providing jobs and income for local people."

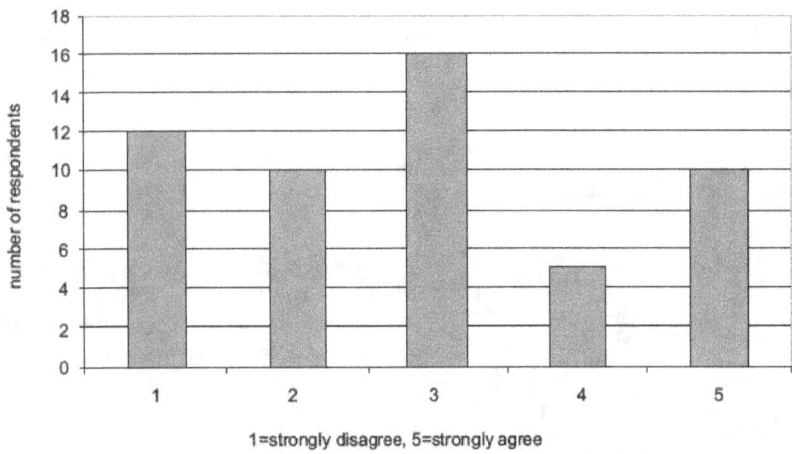

Figure 16—Distribution of responses to: "The decision to develop resources should be based mostly on economic grounds."

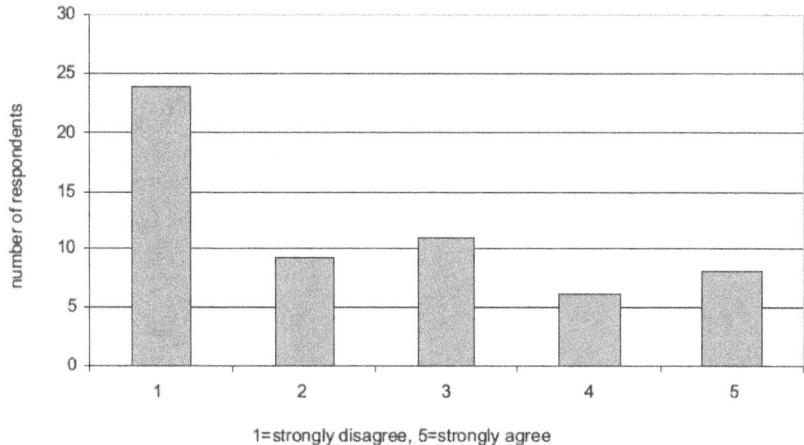

Figure 17—Distribution of responses to: "The government has better places to spend money than devoting resources to a strong conservation program."

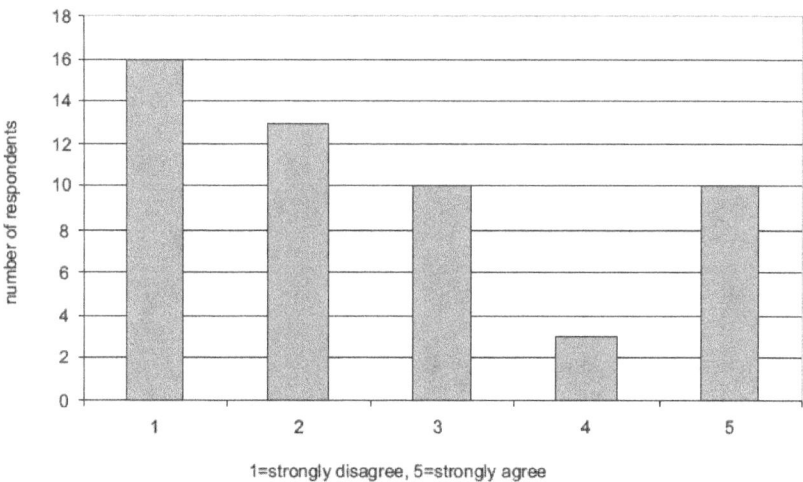

Figure 18—Distribution of responses to: "We should actively harvest more trees to meet the needs of a much larger human population."

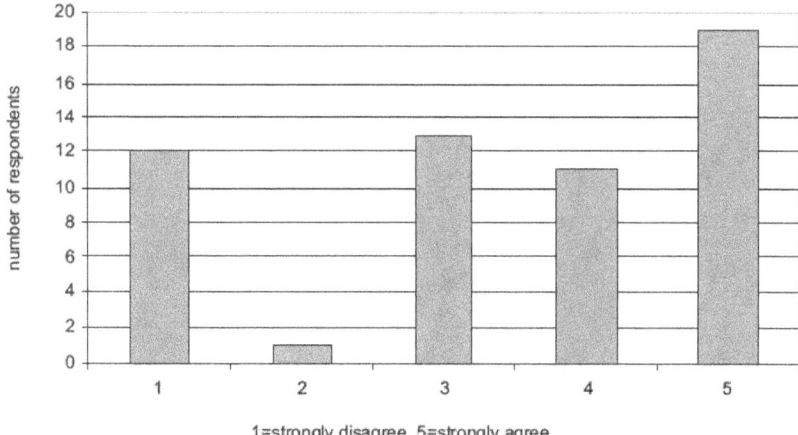

Figure 19—Distribution of responses to: "The main reason for maintaining resources today is so we can develop them in the future if we need to."

Comparison of Region 3 With the Rest of the United States

This final section compares the VOBA results for Region 3 with the results for the rest of the United States. Tables 8 through 11 present the objectives, beliefs about the role of the agency, and customer satisfaction. These are arranged in a manner similar to the previous sections (Core Important Objectives, Other Important Objectives, Unimportant Objectives, and Objectives of Moderate Importance). Table 12 contains comparisons of the Public Lands Values between Region 3 and the rest of the United States. This table is divided into Socially Responsible Individual Values and Socially Responsible Management Values. Discussion will focus on those objectives and values where statistically significant differences exist.

Objectives, Beliefs, and Attitudes

Table 8 reveals that Region 3 does not differ from the rest of the United States regarding the importance of any of the core important objectives, or the beliefs about the role of the USDA Forest Service in fulfilling them. However, they do differ in their evaluation of the performance of the agency in fulfilling two of these objectives: developing volunteer programs to improve the land, and informing the public on the economic value from developing resources. For both of these objectives the evaluation given by Region 3 respondents is less favorable than that given by the rest of the country.

As seen in table 9, Region 3 and the rest of the United States also agree on their ratings of other objectives deemed to be important. Additionally, there are no differences between Region 3 and the rest of the United States in beliefs about the agency's role for these objectives. However, as with the core objectives, Region 3 residents rate agency performance less favorably for protecting ecosystems and wildlife habitat than do respondents from the rest of the United States. Region 3 residents' evaluation of agency performance is also less favorable for the restricting of mineral development on forests and grasslands. For this objective, respondents from Region 3 evaluated the agency's performance to be less than favorable, while the rest of the country finds it favorable.

Table 8--Comparison of objectives, beliefs and attitudes – Region 3 and the rest of the United States.

CORE OBJECTIVES									
	Is this an important objective for you? (1=not at all important, 5=very important)			Do you believe that fulfilling this objective is an appropriate role for the USDA Forest Service? (1=strongly disagree, 5=strongly agree)			How favorably do you view the performance of the USDA Forest Service in fulfilling this objective? (1=very unfavorably, 5=very favorably)		
OBJECTIVE	Region 3	Rest of US	Sig. diff –R3/rest US	Region 3	Rest of US	Sig. diff –R3/rest US	Region 3	Rest of US	Sig. diff –R3/rest US
Conserving and protecting forests and grasslands that are the source of our water resources, such as streams, lakes, and watershed areas.	4.83 0.76[a] 29[b]	4.71 0.75 1298		4.38 1.06 42	4.60 0.83 1364		3.91 1.24 23	3.83 1.10 1171	
Developing volunteer programs to maintain trails and facilities on forests and grasslands (for example, trail maintenance or campground maintenance).	4.39 0.78 23	4.15 1.05 1084		4.17 1.07 29	4.20 1.04 1136		3.55 1.28 20	3.72 1.13 937	
Developing volunteer programs to improve forests and grasslands (for example, tree planting or improving water quality).	4.53 0.84 36	4.54 0.87 1259		4.46 1.10 28	4.51 0.92 1296		2.83 1.27 23	3.74 1.17 932	***
Informing the public on the economic value received by developing our natural resources.	4.16 0.94 25	4.02 1.24 1087		4.08 1.32 24	3.99 1.21 1047		2.69 1.41 26	3.22 1.29 960	*

[a] Standard deviation
[b] Sample size for each item (n). The sample sizes for each item are less than the full 176 sample since each respondent was asked only a portion of the 115 VOBA questions due to time limitations.
*, **, *** mean differences are statistically significant at $\alpha = 0.05$, 0.01, and 0.001 respectively, based on a t-test.

Table 9--Comparison of objectives, beliefs and attitudes – Region 3 and the rest of the United States.

IMPORTANT OBJECTIVES

OBJECTIVE	Is this an important objective for you? (1=not at all important, 5=very important)		Sig. diff –R3/rest US	Do you believe that fulfilling this objective is an appropriate role for the USDA Forest Service? (1=strongly disagree, 5=strongly agree)		Sig. diff –R3/rest US	How favorably do you view the performance of the USDA Forest Service in fulfilling this objective? (1=very unfavorably, 5=very favorably)		Sig. diff –R3/rest US
	Region 3	Rest of US		Region 3	Rest of US		Region 3	Rest of US	
Developing a national policy that guides natural resource development of all kinds (for example, specifies levels of extraction and regulates environmental impacts).	4.31 *1.01[a]* 36[b]	4.22 *1.17* 1259		4.30 *0.92* 20	4.15 *1.15* 1088		3.00 *1.13* 15	3.44 *1.23* 978	
Allowing for diverse uses of forests and grasslands such as grazing, recreation, and wildlife habitat.	4.12 *1.07* 26	4.05 *1.09* 1104		4.00 *1.15* 25	4.05 *1.13* 934		3.84 *1.00* 31	3.67 *1.09* 818	
Protecting ecosystems and wildlife habitats.	4.51 *1.08* 41	4.55 *0.90* 1481		4.47 *1.01* 30	4.56 *0.89* 1292		3.45 *1.41* 31	3.87 *1.10* 1227	*
Increasing law enforcement efforts by public land agencies on public lands.	4.00 *1.08* 18	3.88 *1.22* 944		3.59 *1.26* 22	4.03 *1.16* 952		3.82 *1.33* 17	3.64 *1.22* 775	
Restricting mineral development on forests and grasslands.	4.09 *1.11* 22	3.99 *1.29* 1070		3.77 *1.51* 22	3.94 *1.34* 1101		2.45 *1.15* 29	3.32 *1.36* 899	***
Preserving the ability to have a wilderness experience on forests and grasslands.	4.00 *1.18* 27	4.22 *1.10* 1314		4.22 *1.12* 27	4.22 *1.10* 1332		4.06 *0.90* 33	3.86 *1.03* 1368	
Informing the public about recreation concerns on forests and grasslands such as safety, trail etiquette, and respect for wildlife.	4.39 *1.20* 23	4.55 *0.88* 1144		4.32 *0.99* 22	4.52 *0.90* 1132		3.44 *1.31* 27	3.88 *1.17* 1223	
Making management decisions concerning the use of forests and grasslands at the local level rather than at the national level.	4.05 *1.39* 19	3.98 *1.16* 898		4.17 *0.98* 23	3.93 *1.22* 1080		3.06 *1.48* 16	3.41 *1.26* 789	

[a] Standard deviation
[b] Sample size for each item (n). The sample sizes for each item are less than the full 176 sample since each respondent was asked only a portion of the 115 VOBA questions due to time limitations.
*, **, *** mean differences are statistically significant at α = 0.05, 0.01, and 0.001 respectively, based on a t-test.

Table 10 shows that only one objective determined by the respondents in Region 3 to be unimportant shows a significant difference with the rest of the United States. Although both respondents from Region 3 and those from the rest of the United States find the expansion of off-highway motorized access to be unimportant, the public in Region 3 determined it to be more important than did those from the rest of the United States.

As revealed in table 11, a few items in the group of moderately important objectives show differences between the responses from Region 3 and those of the rest of the country. Respondents within Region 3 believe informing the public on the potential environmental impacts of uses of public lands to be less important than

do respondents within the rest of the United States. However, Region 3's higher standard deviation shows that there are more diverse responses within Region 3 than within the rest of the United States. Region 3 respondents also have differing beliefs about the role of the USDA Forest Service for three of these objectives. Residents in Region 3 feel that designating more wilderness is not an appropriate role for the agency, while residents from the rest of the United States feel that it is a somewhat appropriate role. However, Region 3 views both encouraging collaboration and developing a continuous non-motorized trail system as more appropriate roles for the agency than does the rest of the United States. There are no differences between Region 3 and the rest of the United States for the evaluation of the performance of

Table 10--Comparison of objectives, beliefs and attitudes – Region 3 and the rest of the United States.

UNIMPORTANT OBJECTIVES

OBJECTIVE	Is this an important objective for you? (1=not at all important, 5=very important)		Sig. diff –R3/rest US	Do you believe that fulfilling this objective is an appropriate role for the USDA Forest Service? (1=strongly disagree, 5=strongly agree)		Sig. diff –R3/rest US	How favorably do you view the performance of the USDA Forest Service in fulfilling this objective? (1=very unfavorably, 5=very favorably)		Sig. diff –R3/rest US
	Region 3	Rest of US		Region 3	Rest of US		Region 3	Rest of US	
Expanding access for motorized off-highway vehicles on forests and grasslands (for example, snowmobiling or 4-wheel driving).	2.95 *1.53[a]* 22[b]	2.26 *1.39* 1107	*	2.29 *1.51* 31	2.42 *1.37* 1241		2.40 *1.55* 15	2.96 *1.28* 811	
Making the permitting process easier for some established uses of forests and grasslands such as grazing, logging, mining, and commercial recreation.	2.86 *1.35* 21	2.74 *1.40* 1043		2.76 *1.20* 17	2.66 *1.44* 1117		3.20 *1.42* 15	2.96 *1.27* 752	
Expanding commercial recreation on forests and grasslands (for example, ski areas, guide services, or outfitters).	2.85 *1.39* 20	2.87 *1.30* 1057		2.94 *1.41* 32	3.02 *1.36* 1266		3.70 *0.92* 20	3.36 *1.16* 868	
Developing and maintaining continuous trail systems that cross both public and private land for motorized vehicles such as snowmobiles or ATVs.	2.82 *1.53* 22	2.78 *1.41* 1260		3.21 *1.69* 28	2.80 *1.43* 1095		3.04 *1.40* 24	3.20 *1.19* 913	
Developing new paved roads on forests and grasslands for access for cars and recreational vehicles.	2.42 *1.46* 19	2.39 *1.36* 1091		2.37 *1.47* 27	2.46 *1.41* 1106		3.04 *1.19* 23	3.13 *1.24* 901	

[a] Standard deviation
[b] Sample size for each item (n). The sample sizes for each item are less than the full 176 sample since each respondent was asked only a portion of the 115 VOBA questions due to time limitations.
*, **, *** mean differences are statistically significant at $\alpha = 0.05$, 0.01, and 0.001 respectively, based on a t-test.

the USDA Forest Service in fulfilling these moderately important objectives.

Public Lands Values

For Socially Responsible Individual Values with statistically significant differences (table 12), the means for Region 3 are lower than for the rest of the United States. This suggests that there is a lower level of environmental orientation within Region 3 than for the rest of the United States. Additionally, for the one Socially Responsible Management Value statement where Region 3 shows a significant difference, the response from this Region is lower than from the rest of the country. These statements are worded so that a higher response indicates that a respondent values the extraction and use of natural resources more highly. So, while Region 3 respondents exhibit a lower level of environmental orientation on the Individual Values, they also exhibit a lower preference for human-centered uses of forests and grasslands when responding to the Management Values (although this is demonstrated by only one statistically different statement). While there is not a statistically significant difference, Region 3 residents are strongly of the opinion that the United States government should not subsidize the development of public lands.

Table 11--Comparison of objectives, beliefs and attitudes – Region 3 and the rest of the United States.

OBJECTIVES OF MODERATE IMPORTANCE

OBJECTIVE	Is this an important objective for you? (1=not at all important, 5=very important)		Sig. diff –R3/rest US	Do you believe that fulfilling this objective is an appropriate role for the USDA Forest Service? (1=strongly disagree, 5=strongly agree)		Sig. diff –R3/rest US	How favorably do you view the performance of the USDA Forest Service in fulfilling this objective? (1=very unfavorably, 5=very favorably)		Sig. diff –R3/rest US
	Region 3	Rest of US		Region 3	Rest of US		Region 3	Rest of US	
Preserving the natural resources of forests and grasslands through such policies as no timber harvesting or no mining.	3.91 *1.38[a]* 23[b]	4.15 *1.22* 1336		4.06 *1.18* 31	4.13 *1.26* 1312		3.42 *1.36* 26	3.60 *1.23* 1143	
Restricting timber harvesting and grazing on forests and grasslands.	3.88 *1.62* 24	3.96 *1.25* 1118		3.74 *1.44* 35	3.95 *1.30* 1036		2.96 *1.26* 23	3.31 *1.29* 923	
Preserving the cultural uses of forests and grasslands by Native Americans and Native Hispanics such as firewood gathering, her/berry/plant gathering, and ceremonial access.	3.81 *1.30* 31	3.78 *1.29* 1323		3.65 *1.50* 23	3.65 *1.31* 1440		3.60 *0.91* 25	3.39 *1.23* 995	
Designating more wilderness areas on public land that stops access for development and motorized uses.	3.80 *1.44* 41	3.85 *1.29* 1034		2.94 *1.68* 17	3.67 *1.40* 1074	*	2.95 *1.24* 21	3.30 *1.24* 880	
Providing natural resources from forests and grasslands to support communities dependent on grazing, mining, or timber harvesting.	3.54 *1.65* 26	3.55 *1.32* 1080		3.05 *1.33* 22	3.26 *1.36* 1054		3.28 *1.24* 25	3.35 *1.16* 1019	
Encouraging collaboration between groups in order to share information concerning uses of forests and grasslands.	3.90 *1.17* 20	4.22 *1.09* 1046		4.63 *0.71* 24	4.19 *1.05* 1043	*	3.81 *1.08* 21	3.56 *1.14* 880	
Using public advisory committees to advise on public land management issues.	3.57 *1.31* 23	3.85 *1.16* 947		3.89 *1.23* 18	3.88 *1.15* 909		2.82 *1.25* 11	3.33 *1.18* 709	
Informing the public on the potential environmental impacts of all uses associated with forests and grasslands.	3.90 *1.48* 21	4.40 *0.98* 1151	*	4.32 *0.99* 25	4.45 *0.93* 1110		3.57 *1.38* 23	3.41 *1.27* 990	
Designating some existing recreation trails for specific use (for example, creating separate trails for snowmobiling and cross-country skiing or for mountain biking and horseback riding).	3.67 *1.33* 27	3.68 *1.32* 1093		3.57 *1.29* 21	3.93 *1.17* 1060		3.17 *0.99* 18	3.58 *1.18* 946	
Developing and maintaining continuous trail systems that cross both public and private land for non-motorized recreation such as hiking or cross-country skiing.	3.67 *1.35* 15	3.72 *1.27* 1118		4.36 *1.19* 25	3.66 *1.30* 1100	**	3.50 *1.19* 22	3.59 *1.15* 898	
Paying an entry fee that goes to support public land.	3.44 *1.34[a]* 18[b]	3.60 *1.30* 917		3.41 *1.40* 22	3.65 *1.29* 954		3.45 *1.15* 20	3.51 *1.24* 795	
Allowing public land managers to trade public land for private lands (for example to eliminate private property within public land boundaries or to acquire unique areas of land).	3.40 *1.64* 15	3.10 *1.38* 823		3.40 *1.10* 20	3.21 *1.39* 846		2.95 *1.17* 22	3.15 *1.22* 773	
Increasing the total number of acres in the public land system.	3.38 *1.32* 29	3.68 *1.34* 936		3.86 *1.24* 21	3.82 *1.33* 932		3.38 *1.45* 13	3.41 *1.21* 796	

[a] Standard deviation
[b] Sample size for each item (n). The sample sizes for each item are less than the full 176 sample since each respondent was asked only a portion of the 115 VOBA questions due to time limitations.
*, **, *** mean differences are statistically significant at $\alpha = 0.05$, 0.01, and 0.001 respectively, based on a t-test.

Table 12--Comparison of values - Region 3 and the rest of the United States.

SOCIALLY RESPONSIBLE INDIVIDUAL VALUES			
VALUES *(1=strongly disagree, 5=strongly agree)*	Region 3	Rest of US	Significant difference between Region 3 and the rest of the US
I am glad there are national forests even if I never get to see them.	4.69 *0.78[a]* 52[b]	4.75 *0.73* 1997	
Donating time or money to worthy causes is important to me.	4.17 *0.99* 53	4.19 *1.02* 1778	
Manufacturers should be encouraged to use recycled materials in their manufacturing and processing operations.	4.63 *1.00* 40	4.65 *0.79* 1958	
Future generations should be just as important as the current one in the decisions about public lands.	4.52 *1.03* 61	4.59 *0.84* 2045	
I am willing to make personal sacrifices for the sake of slowing down pollution.	4.15 *1.10* 40	4.37 *0.94* 1794	
Consumers should be interested in the environmental consequences of the products they purchase.	4.15 *1.14* 39	4.49 *0.89* 1813	*
Forests have a right to exist for their own sake, regardless of human concerns and uses.	4.17 *1.15* 42	4.11 *1.18* 1910	
People can think public lands are valuable even if they do not actually go there themselves.	4.31 *1.17* 51	4.63 *0.82* 1772	**
I am willing to stop buying products from companies that pollute the environment even though it might be inconvenient.	3.98 *1.26* 43	3.96 *1.16* 1823	
People should be concerned about how our public lands are used.	4.16 *1.28* 37	4.67 *0.77* 1779	***
The whole pollution issue has never upset me, I feel it's somewhat overrated. [c]	3.84 *1.36* 45	3.74 *1.40* 1806	
I have often thought that if we could just get by with a little less there would be more left for future generations.	3.80 *1.38* 49	4.05 *1.21* 1703	
People should urge their friends to limit their use of products made from scarce resources.	3.63 *1.40* 43	4.14 *1.11* 1989	**
Natural resources must be preserved even if people must do without some products.	3.71 *1.41* 58	4.10 *1.16* 1957	*
Wildlife, plants, and humans have equal rights to live and grow.	3.90 *1.49* 49	4.15 *1.27* 1752	
I would be willing to pay five dollars more each time I use public lands for recreational purposes (for example, hiking, camping, hunting).	3.22 *1.52[a]* 59[b]	3.53 *1.45* 2152	
I would be willing to sign a petition for an environmental cause.	3.45 *1.60* 47	3.89 *1.34* 1735	*

SOCIALLY RESPONSIBLE MANAGEMENT VALUES

VALUES *(1=strongly disagree, 5=strongly agree)*	Region 3	Rest of US	Significant difference between Region 3 and the rest of the US
The Federal government should subsidize the development and leasing of public lands to companies.	1.79 *1.18* 47	2.14 *1.37* 2284	
The primary use of forests should be for products that are useful to humans.	2.37 *1.22* 71	2.69 *1.43* 2476	
I think that the public land managers are doing an adequate job of protecting natural resources from being overused.	3.04 *1.38* 47	3.09 *1.18* 2117	
The decision to develop resources should be based mostly on economic grounds.	2.83 *1.40* 53	2.69 *1.35* 2232	
The most important role for the public lands is providing jobs and income for local people.	2.53 *1.40* 68	2.93 *1.40* 2512	*
The government has better places to spend money than devoting resources to a strong conservation program.	2.40 *1.46* 58	2.25 *1.31* 2292	
We should actively harvest more trees to meet the needs of a much larger human population.	2.58 *1.47* 52	2.57 *1.53* 2291	
The main reason for maintaining resources today is so we can develop them in the future if we need to.	3.43 *1.51* 56	3.71 *1.37* 2256	

[a] Standard deviation

[b] Sample size for each item (n). The sample sizes for each item are less than the full 176 sample since each respondent was asked only a portion of the 115 VOBA questions due to time limitations.

*, **, *** mean differences are statistically significant at $\alpha = 0.05$, 0.01, and 0.001 respectively, based on a t-test.

Appendix

Survey Design and Implementation

The design of the VOBA survey began with focus groups and interviews. Between September 1999 and June 2000 over 80 focus groups and individual interviews were conducted across the lower 48 states. These efforts concentrated on three topics; 1) issues related to the use of public lands in general and forests and rangelands in particular, 2) the objectives (or goals) of the group (or individual) regarding the use, management, and conservation of the forests and rangelands, and 3) the role of the Forest Service in the use, management, and conservation of the forests and rangelands.

Based upon the results of the focus groups and interviews, an objectives hierarchy was constructed for each group of stakeholders. These hierarchies indicate what each group or individual was attempting to achieve, and how they would achieve each goal or objective. These objectives ranged from the abstract strategic level to the more specific or applied means level. The means level objectives are at the bottom of the hierarchy, while the strategic objective is at the top. Fundamental objectives between the means level and the strategic level completed the hierarchies. Therefore, the strategic level objective is an abstract objective that can be achieved by more specific fundamental level objectives, which are in turn achieved by means level objectives. (See figure 1.)

Each of the objectives hierarchies was confirmed with its respective group so as to ensure that it accurately reflected the group's goals and objectives. A combined objectives hierarchy was then constructed that included all the objectives stated by each group or individual interviewed. The result was a hierarchy that covered five strategic level objectives related to access, preservation/conservation, commodity development, education, and natural resource management. These 5 strategic level objectives were supported by 30 fundamental objectives.

The 30 fundamental level objectives were used to develop 30 objectives statements that were used in the National Survey of Recreation and the Environment (NSRE). The NSRE is a national survey administered via telephone interviews. The 30 objectives statements were divided into 5 groups based upon the strategic level objectives the focus groups had identified. During the telephone interviews, each respondent was asked one statement from each of the five strategic level groups to obtain a statistically valid sample for each statement and for each strategic level group.

As noted above, the survey of the American public's values, objectives, beliefs and attitudes was conducted as a module within the NSRE. Although questions about respondents' recreation behavior comprise the bulk of the interview, the results presented here are based solely on the questions in the VOBA Module of the survey and the demographic questions. Participants were asked to respond to the VOBA questions using a five-point scale. The objectives questions are anchored with 1=not at all important to 5=very important. Beliefs are anchored with 1=strongly disagree to 5=strongly agree, and attitudes are anchored with 1=very unfavorable to 5=very favorable. Each of these 3 scales consists of 30 items. The 25 items in the "values" scale are anchored with 1=strongly disagree and 5=strongly agree.

Reverse Scoring

When the VOBA survey was designed, care was taken to avoid the appearance of an instrument that was biased toward or against a specific position. To do this the "direction" of the scale varied. For example, for one item a "strongly agree" response might indicate a conservation/preservation orientation, while for another item the same response might indicate a development orientation. While this is useful to increase the acceptance of the instrument and subsequent response rates, it creates problems when items with the opposite direction are grouped.

To compare two or more items that have opposite directions, it is necessary to make all the items move in the same direction. For example, suppose we want to examine the overall preference for sweets as indicated by the preference for ice cream and pie. We have two scale items. For each, 1 indicates "strongly disagree" and 5 indicates "strongly agree" as in the Public Lands Values scale. To avoid the appearance of bias toward or against sweets, the two items move in opposite directions: "I like ice cream" and "I don't like pie." Clearly a person who likes all sweets will answer 5 to the first item and 1 to the second. Conversely, someone who does not like sweets will answer 1 to the first and 5 to the second. If these items are grouped, it would be more useful to a research if the two items are scored to indicate preference for sweets either with a higher response for both items (or lower, either way would work). So, to re-score, we choose one of the items, in this example we'll choose the second, and reverse the scoring. So, answer of 5 to "I don't like pie" becomes a 1 (and we can reword the item as "I like pie"). An answer of 4 becomes 2, 3 remains the same (neutral), 2 becomes 4, and 1 becomes 5. This in effect creates a new item that corresponds in direction to "I like ice cream." Now we have an indication of each respondent's preference for sweets. Higher numbers for each item indicate a higher preference for sweets, and lower numbers indicate lower preference. A similar re-scoring was done for certain items in the VOBA to more accurately characterize overall preferences for item groups.